Eagle
in the Sky

Written by Fay Robinson

CelebrationPress
An Imprint of ScottForesman

Do you recognize this bird? You've probably never seen one in the sky, but you may have noticed its picture on things you see every day. This is the American bald eagle.

Many bald eagles live here.

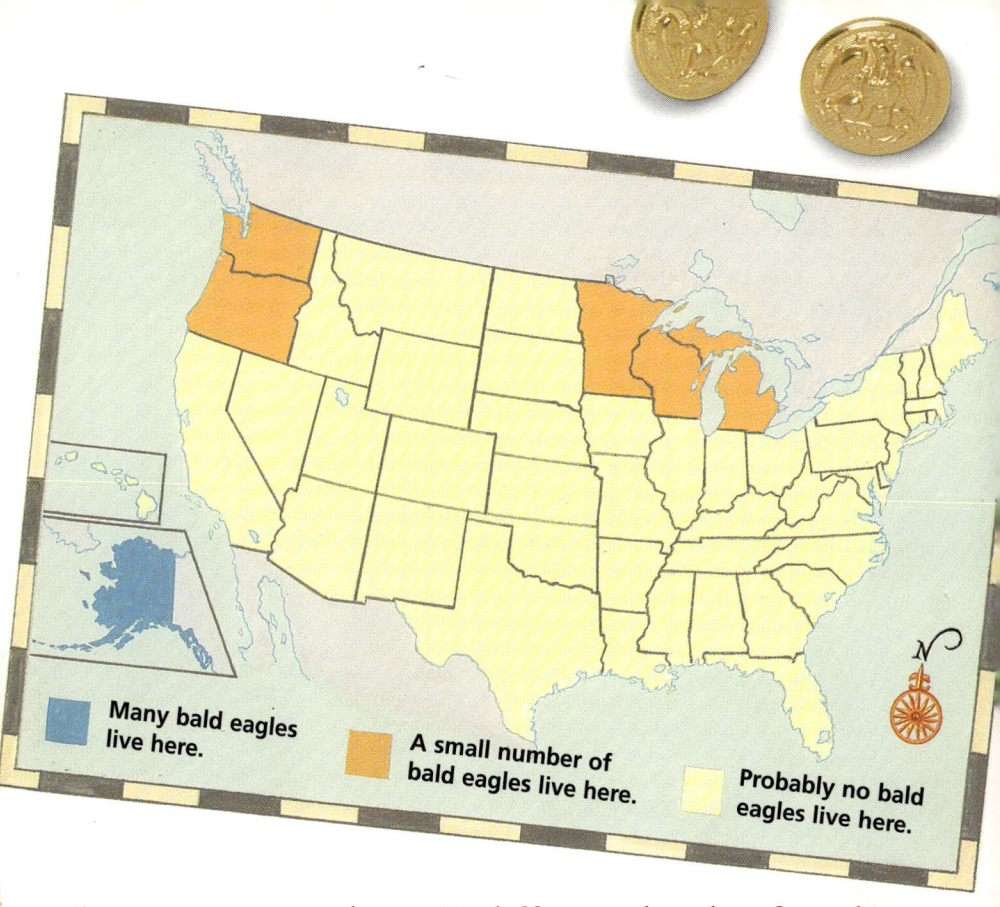

A small number of bald eagles live here.

Probably no bald eagles live here.

There are more than 50 different kinds of eagles, but only the bald eagle makes its home in North America and nowhere else.

The bald eagle is one of the largest birds in the world. Its body can be three feet long!

Sharp eyes can see as far as a mile away.

Beak is 2 inches long.

Wingspan is up to 8 feet across.

Body has over
7,000 feathers.

Talons have
needle-sharp points.

5

Bald eagles are strong and powerful. They can fly at speeds of 45 miles per hour — faster than cars on city streets. They can travel up to 200 miles in a day.

7

Bald eagles are almost always found near water.
That's because fish is their favorite food.

When a bald eagle goes fishing, it uses its excellent eyesight to spot a fish in the water. Then it swoops down, grabs the fish in its talons, and carries it away.

Eagles build their nest high in a treetop. They use moss, sticks, and even animal bones! Often, eagle pairs return to the same nest every year, making it bigger each time.

11

Females usually lay two eggs. The newly hatched eaglets are all brown. As they grow, their eyes, beaks, and feet turn bright yellow. White head and tail feathers replace the brown ones. One day they will look just like their parents.

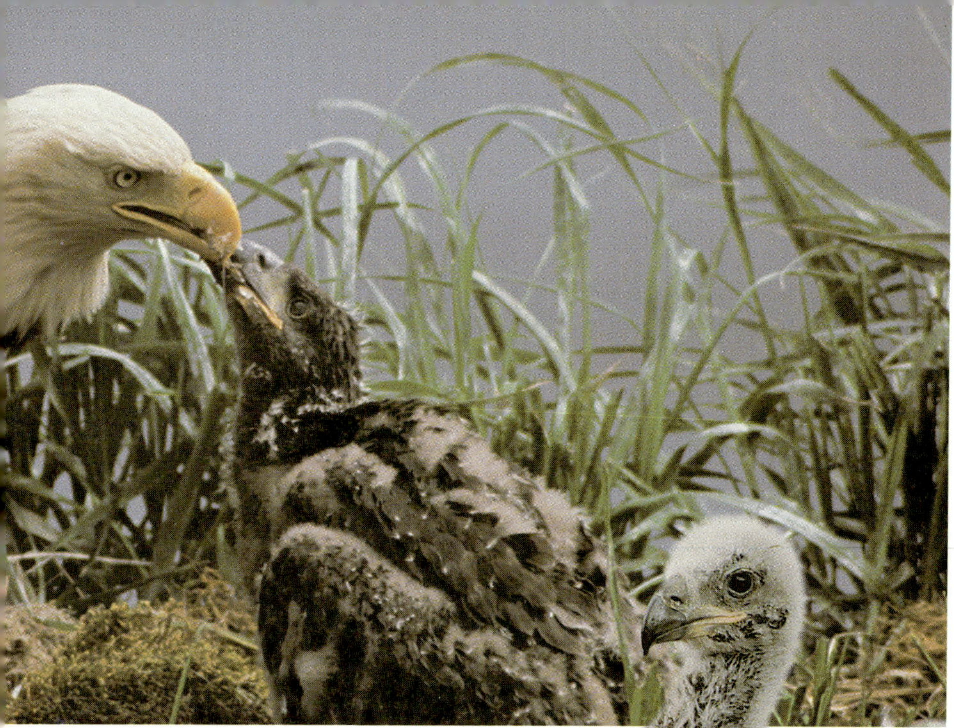

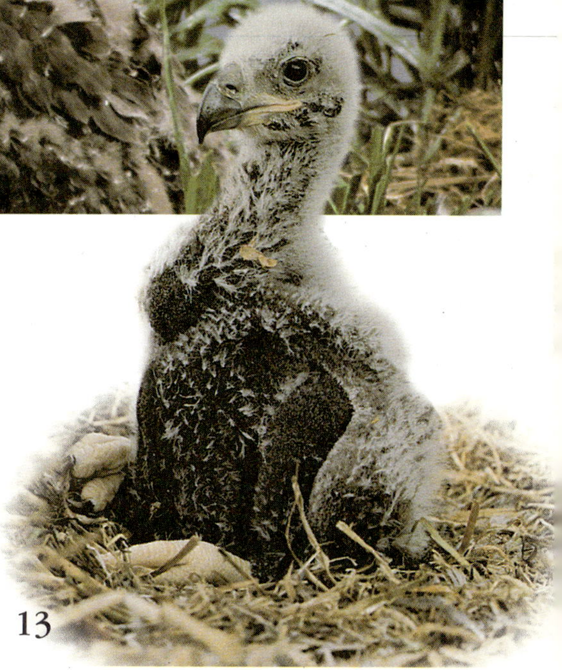

The bald eagle is an endangered animal. This means that we must take care of those that are left and the places where they live.

▲Some sprays are harmful to eagles.

People have cut down some of ▶ the trees eagles need for nesting.

14

15

Today people work hard to help eagles. Maybe, someday, there will be eagles in the sky all across the country.